JOHN COX

Light
to the
Nations

**An Advent course based on
the prophecies of Isaiah**

www.kevinmayhew.com

First published in Great Britain in 2013 by Kevin Mayhew Ltd
Buxhall, Stowmarket, Suffolk IP14 3BW
Tel: +44 (0) 1449 737978 Fax: +44 (0) 1449 737834
E-mail: info@kevinmayhewltd.com

www.kevinmayhew.com

9 8 7 6 5 4 3 2 1 0

ISBN 978 1 84867 642 8
Catalogue No. 1501402

Cover design by Justin Minns
© Images used under licence from Shutterstock Inc.
Edited by Nicki Copeland
Typeset by Richard Weaver

Printed and bound in Great Britain

Contents

About the author

John Cox recently retired as Diocesan Director of Education in the diocese of St Edmundsbury and Ipswich, where he had previously been Archdeacon of Sudbury. He served as a parish priest in Lancashire, Birmingham and London and for eight years was Director of Ordinands in the Diocese of Southwark. He now concentrates on school governorship, writing and editing. It doesn't leave him as much time for golf as he would like.

Introduction

I am the Lord, I have called you in righteousness,
I have taken you by the hand and kept you;
I have given you as a covenant to the people,
a light to the nations,
to open the eyes that are blind,
to bring out the prisoners from the dungeon,
from the prison those who sit in darkness.

Isaiah 42:6-7

It is too light a thing that you should be my servant
to raise up the tribes of Jacob
and to restore the survivors of Israel;
I will give you as a light to the nations,
that my salvation may reach to the end of the earth . . .
I have kept you and given you
as a covenant to the people,
to establish the land,
to apportion the desolate heritages;
saying to the prisoners, 'Come out',
to those who are in darkness, 'Show yourselves.'

Isaiah 49:6, 8-9

The Spirit of the Lord God is upon me,
because the Lord has anointed me;
he has sent me to bring good news to the oppressed,
to bind up the broken-hearted,
to proclaim liberty to the captives,
and release to the prisoners;

> to proclaim the year of the Lord's favour,
> and the day of vengeance of our God;
> to comfort all who mourn.

Isaiah 61:1-2

When he came to Nazareth, where he had been brought up, he went to the synagogue on the sabbath day, as was his custom. He stood up to read, and the scroll of the prophet Isaiah was given to him. He unrolled the scroll and found the place where it was written:

> 'The Spirit of the Lord is upon me,
> because he has anointed me to bring good news to the poor.
> He has sent me to proclaim release to the captives,
> and recovery of sight to the blind,
> to let the oppressed go free,
> to proclaim the year of the Lord's favour.'

And he rolled up the scroll, gave it back to the attendant, and sat down. The eyes of all in the synagogue were fixed on him. Then he began to say to them, 'Today this scripture has been fulfilled in your hearing.' All spoke well of him and were amazed at the gracious words that came from his mouth.

Luke 4:16-22

Light amidst the darkness

A child's fear of the dark is deeply rooted in the human psyche. The dangers that have surrounded human beings from earliest times were amplified by the absence of light. Without light, the apparent safety of a cave could erupt with unexpected dangers lurking in the shadows. The darkness of night and the darkness of winter were natural contexts for anxiety and fear. Experience and imagination populated them with known and unknown dangers that threatened immediate attack or longer-term threat.

It is little wonder that the natural cycle of dawn and dusk, day and night, summer and winter gave rise to religious practices, both primitive and sophisticated. Among the most elaborate were the religious beliefs and practices that emerged in the Middle East, and especially in Egypt where the sun god, Ra, was the major deity. Nut, the goddess of the night sky, was among the most ancient of the gods, and was sometimes pictured as swallowing the sun's disk at dusk and expelling it at dawn. In more northerly climes it was the cycle of the seasons that encouraged rituals around the time of the winter solstice when the days were shortest and the sun at its lowest. There were other rites, too, that marked the return of the sun and the renewal of life after the dead of winter. Chaos and death were the overarching threats that dwelt in the darkness, only to be expelled by the coming of the light.

These deeply felt regular anxieties fed not only the spiritual imagination but found expression in the imagery of everyday life. The dark is a symbol of ignorance, and we speak of the Enlightenment to refer to the time when, in the western world, scientific and technical knowledge advanced under the guidance of Reason. 'I've seen the light' is how someone might describe either a gradual insight or a sudden discovery. We speak of a truth 'dawning' on us. If we find it hard to reach a solution to a problem, we look for someone to 'throw light' on the situation. We look for the light at the end of the tunnel, and the weight of depression is also a darkness that envelopes and suffocates the spirit from which we seek relief, a new dawn. A loved one might be described as 'the light of my life'.

Existential, religious and everyday experiences work together to give rich levels of meaning to the vocabulary of light and darkness. This is seen powerfully within the Christian faith and practice. The candles that at one level were merely a practical way of dispelling darkness and allowing priests to read the liturgy are also the signs of the presence of the Spirit, a symbol of the risen Christ, a tangible expression of the prayer of the heart. The living flame is more than light; it is an image of vitality and hope. In Catholic churches, the Sanctuary light burns to signify the presence of the holy sacrament.

The Bible is full of the imagery of light and dark, and in the work of creation the Lord made the two great lights and 'saw that it was good' (Genesis 1:18). To the psalmist, the Lord is light and salvation (Psalm 27:1), and his word is a lamp to the feet (Psalm 119:105). For the writer of Proverbs, it was God's law that gave light (Proverbs 6:23). The prophet Isaiah called upon the people to 'walk in the light of the Lord' (Isaiah 2:5), while Amos warned the people that the day of the Lord would be a day of darkness, not light (Amos 5:18), a day of judgement, not rescue.

In the New Testament, it is in John's Gospel that we most often find images of light – the light that shines in the spiritual darkness. The tragedy was that people seemed to prefer the darkness, while the good news was that the true light has dawned for all (John 1:9, 3:19). The people are called to believe and to walk in the light while the light is present (John 12:35-36). Most significantly, it is Jesus who is identified as the light of the world, the true light (John 8:12). Holman Hunt's famous picture captures something of this rich symbolism of what the dark means, and the promise of him who is the light of the world.

These are just a few of the threads that come together in an Advent course that speaks of light. Advent itself is set in the Church's calendar in the dark winter days that look forward to and long for the coming of the light – the birth of the Christ child, the light of the world. It gives Christian expression to an old winter festival which had its own longings for the light. It is a preparation of the spirit to welcome the coming of the one whose light is rescue, salvation from all that the darkness holds. But the darkness and the deeds of darkness have first to be recognised for what they are, to be repented of, turned from, so that one might delight in walking in the light.

So in the promise of light there is also judgement upon the darkness – the darkness within each one of us and within the society of which we are part. Advent is a season of penitence, a purple season, a preparation season. The light will not be recognised for what it truly is, will not be welcomed and lived by without such preparation. That such a season comes round on an annual basis reminds us that the life of faith, the walk with Christ who is the light, is not a single event but a journey with its delights and its doubts, its times of closeness to our Lord and its times when we feel far away. It is a time of checking out our spiritual well-being, a time to reflect on the places where the light has not yet reached and where the darkness has crept in.

The prophecy of Isaiah

It is the prophet Isaiah who uses the phrase 'light to the nations'. In Isaiah 42:6 he says, 'I have given you as a covenant to the people, a light to the nations,' and in chapter

49:6, 'I will give you as a light to the nations.' The prophet is recording what he understands to be the commission of God to his servant. Over the years there has been plenty of discussion, and a considerable amount of ink used, in the attempt to identify who the servant is. The suggestions range from the prophet himself, or another individual, to the whole people of Israel. The early Church interpreted these passages as a prophecy about Jesus. In this it may have been following Jesus' own identification of himself with the Suffering Servant (Isaiah 53; Luke 22:37).

The prophecies come from that section of the book of Isaiah which is generally known as Second Isaiah (chapters 40–55). Probably pronounced by a single prophet following in the tradition of Isaiah of Jerusalem, they come from the period of the Exile in Babylon around 540 BC. By chapter 49, Babylon itself was facing defeat by the Persian empire under Cyrus, and the prophet was concerned with preparing the people for their return to Palestine. It is therefore a period of emerging from turmoil, one in which there was good reason for hope and in which the people were called to renew their faith in the promises of God. His rescue act (salvation) not only offered the people the possibility of restoration to their homeland, but it would also indicate his faithfulness and be a call to them to live as a beacon of that faithfulness and power to all the nations.

A more individual interpretation would mean that the prophet himself is to be a beacon of light showing, not only to God's people but to all the world, the saving purposes of God. Scholars point out that the word that has been translated 'light' – a vivid image that we can readily appreciate – may have actually meant 'covenant'. This would have made the phrase, 'I have appointed you to be a covenant.' Such an expression would be unique but not impossible. God's covenant with Abraham had been sealed by the sacrifice of an animal and a flaming torch moving between its divided parts (Genesis 15:17). The reference would therefore be that the Servant is called to be the very means of establishing the covenant, not merely its mediator, as Moses had been in the giving of the Sinai covenant. But whether 'light' or 'covenant', the point to emphasise is that it is for all people. God's purpose was not restricted to the rescue of his own people from exile, and in their turn they were to see their own role not only as the recipients of salvation but the proclaimers of it for the well-being of others.

Isaiah 49:6 is more certainly from the second of the so-called Servant Songs. It is a poem in which the Servant speaks of his commissioning from birth and of being given a message that is both for Israel and beyond. He confesses failure, but in his utter reliance upon God he learns of the great scope of his role in God's purposes. Light and salvation arc to be brought to all people. As exiles are freed to return to Jerusalem from all over the world, and as the returning journey is made easy by a caring God, it is as though the whole of nature rejoices and celebrates (Isaiah 49:8-13).

Isaiah 61:1ff takes us into the third section of the book of Isaiah. Here the prophecies are more likely to have been the product of a 'school of prophets' working in the tradition of the earlier Isaiah(s). The context has moved from Babylon to Palestine in a period around 500 BC after the return of the first exiles and the rebuilding of the Temple. Some of the early enthusiasm and high expectation had faded. The high hopes had been overcome by economic difficulties, and there was antagonism between those who had returned and those who had stayed in Palestine during the Exile. People had begun to doubt the promises of God, and society was far from the utopian ideal that had been anticipated.

The prophecy, while being primarily about the prophet, goes beyond the immediate present and future and looks to the New Age which is the fulfilment and goal of history and in which the people of God fulfil the role of the Servant, of the Davidic king, and take on the priestly role for all nations. The task of the people is to bring light into the social, economic and personal darkness. They are to be proclaimers of the good news that God's promise will not fail, that there is rescue for the oppressed, that light will be given to eyes that cannot see, that a time of prosperity and spiritual well-being is coming through the activity of God.

Jesus, the bringer of light

The future announced by the prophet was a long time coming. In many ways, of course, it is still to come. But through the teaching and the life, death and resurrection of Jesus, Christians have come to believe that the New Age has at least been inaugurated.

Jesus himself made few personal claims, and it is not entirely clear in what terms he saw himself – the Gospels bring their own interpretation to that. But it is certainly possible that he did identify himself in some way with the Servant figure in the prophecies of Isaiah. Even in the synagogue in Nazareth he did not make that direct identification, and focused more on the coming of the day of the Lord than on his own role. But that he had a part to play, a unique part, does seem clear.

For Luke, Jesus' return to Nazareth marked the beginning of his public ministry of preaching, teaching and healing.

From the outset, his message was radical, but he was not out to destroy the religion of his ancestors. It was, says Luke, his habit to attend the regular worship of the synagogue. The changes he wished to make were not by destruction but through transformation. Like the prophets of old, he wanted a people and a religion that reflected a fuller understanding of the God he called Father and a more faithful relationship of the people with that God. He did that from within Judaism, the faith he had been brought up in and was part of.

Synagogue

The origins of the synagogue are not entirely clear, but they most probably emerged around the time of the Exile. Its basic meaning is 'a place of gathering', and it came to be distinctive of Jewish worship. In the time of the Diaspora, when Jews lived far from the Temple and were not able to participate in its worship, the synagogue provided a place for both worship and the discussion of civil affairs. It did not replace worship at the Temple but existed alongside it.

Unlike worship in the Temple, synagogue worship centred not around sacrifice but around the reading of the Torah and prayers. Scrolls of the Law and the Prophets were kept in a portable ark facing the door of the synagogue and on fast days were processed. The chief officers of the synagogue sat on chairs in front of the ark, and the men and women sat separately. The ruler of the synagogue was responsible for the affairs of the synagogue and, like other officials, was a layman. It was the attendant's responsibility to oversee the teaching of the children, to punish offenders by scourging and to bring the scroll to the reader during worship.

A service could only take place if ten men were present. It began with a recitation of a statement of faith (the Shema) and the 18 benedictions and prayers. There was then a reading from the Law followed by a reading from the Prophets which would be expounded. Any person deemed to be competent could read and expound the Scriptures. Readings may have been fixed according to a lectionary, or it could have been that Jesus requested a particular scroll. The service closed with a benediction.

It says something about Jesus' reputation even prior to his public ministry that he was considered to be a suitable person to read and expound the Scriptures. On this occasion he is not reported as having preached a sermon. He read the passage and then merely commented upon it: 'Today this scripture has been fulfilled in your hearing' (Luke 4:21). If the interpretation of the Isaiah passage given above is correct – that it was originally about the prophet himself – Jesus is saying that he is the re-enactment of the spirit-filled and anointed messenger whose mission is divinely authorised and empowered – a mission that brings salvation to all people.

There is a slight awkwardness in Luke's reporting of the people's reaction. Initially there is admiration and wonder, but as Jesus continues to speak (the content of which is not directly related to the Isaiah passage), that very quickly turns to hostility. Only Luke records the content of what Jesus preached in a synagogue, although the other Gospels do record that he did it (Mark 1:21, 27, 39; 3:1 cf Matthew 4:23, 9:35). The pattern of reading the Scripture, expounding it in terms of the fulfilment of God's time of salvation and then the rejection of the preacher is one we find in accounts of the apostles' preaching in Acts (13:17ff, 17:2ff).

The course and how it might be used

This short Advent course is suitable for either private use or by groups. Its five sessions are based on the five main sections of the task laid upon the spirit-filled and anointed servant of the Isaiah passage that was read out by Jesus in the Nazareth synagogue and which were understood to be fulfilled in his ministry and person. They are:

- bringing good news to the poor
- proclaiming release to captives
- the recovery of sight to the blind
- letting the oppressed go free
- proclaiming the year of the Lord's favour.

Each section begins with an introduction that sets out some reflections on the topic. If the course is being used in a group, this material should be read before the meeting of the group. These introductions offer some background material, wider scriptural references and thoughts about the implications for today.

Suggestions are then made for the content of the session. Each one follows a similar pattern: gathering together, sharing the word, exploring the message, going out. As well as a passage to focus the thoughts, there are prayers, suggestions for discussion and/or activities, and a time of reflection. These are all intended to be helpful suggestions rather than rigorous requirements. Groups work differently and have different priorities. Some like plenty of discussion; others may prefer more activity. For some, music can be a help; others prefer silence. A time of shared and spontaneous prayer may be the preferred way for some groups; others may want something more formal. The group should feel free to use the material as a stimulus, not feel constrained by it like a straitjacket. It is a resource, not a rule book!

Some practical considerations

The weeks leading up to Christmas offer an obvious period when a group might meet, but it is also an increasingly busy time as Christmas approaches and churches often have lots going on. Arrangements should be flexible to fit in with the life of the church and of group members. Rather than attempting to get through the course in Advent, it might be better either to start a few weeks early and meet fortnightly, or to split the five sessions either side of Christmas. Light is a suitable theme for Epiphany as well as for Advent, leading up to Candlemas.

Groups will normally find it helpful for each member to have a copy of the course book and also to bring a Bible to each session. A case can be made for using one version of the Bible or for drawing upon different translations. Different versions can sometimes bring a richness in drawing out the meaning of a passage, as long as this doesn't distract the group into long discussions about the accuracy of a particular version. The passages in this book are all from the New Revised Standard Version.

Groups will, of course, have to decide where to meet – in a small meeting room, in church, in someone's home. Some groups prefer to stick to one venue; others like to move around to different people's homes. Whatever the setting, it needs to be warm and reasonably comfortable (though not soporific), without undue distractions from other parts of the building – especially important if meeting in a church where other people are also meeting.

There is always the question of refreshments. Arrangements could range from meeting for a meal together before the session to a cup of tea either at the beginning or end. If the group is circulating to different homes it is advisable to keep refreshments reasonably simple so that this does not become a matter of competition!

If music is going to be used, then suitable equipment needs to be set up beforehand.

If the group meets during Advent, it might wish to mark the weeks with the lighting of candles, perhaps in the traditional form of an Advent wreath. This will have one red candle for each week of Advent and a white one in the middle to represent Christ coming as the light of the world, the light to the nations. Groups may wish to sing or recite at the lighting of the candle. Suggestions of suitable songs and hymns are offered in the Appendix.

Most groups will have a leader, who may or may not be the host. There may be one leader for all five sessions or the group might decide to have a different leader for each session. The leader has the responsibility of steering the group through the session, without dominating, of ensuring that the agreed length of time is kept to, and of helping every person to be as involved as they wish to be. Not everyone wants to make lots of contributions, and silence does not necessarily mean not being involved. Occasionally a group will have a member who wants to monopolise the session. Handling this can take sensitivity, but it is up to the leader to ensure that one person doesn't take over so that others have little chance to make their point.

The points for discussion are provided as a series of suggestions across the main themes raised by the week's topic. It is unlikely that the group will either want to attempt all of them or have time to do so. It will be the responsibility of the leader, together with the group, to make these choices.

As part of the reflection on the discussion, it is suggested that verses from a suitable hymn might be read (either aloud or silently) and/or sung. The Appendix provides a number of hymns that have especial relevance for the topics of the different sessions.

NB For Session 5, members are asked to take with them a recent newspaper.

Week one

Good news to the poor

Introduction

The Spirit of the Lord God is upon me,
because the Lord has anointed me;
he has sent me to bring good news to the oppressed.

Isaiah 61:1

'The Spirit of the Lord is upon me, because he has anointed
me to bring good news to the poor.'

Luke 4:18

The Christian message is summed up as 'gospel' or 'good
news'. Jesus, we are told, came to proclaim good news. The
disciples and apostles preached good news. The Church is
committed to share good news.

But what is the good news? Saint Mark begins his Gospel
with these words: 'The beginning of the good news [gospel]
of Jesus Christ, the Son of God' (Mark 1:1). Ask Christians
today and some will say that it is the good news of
forgiveness and salvation that God offers us through the life,
death and resurrection of Jesus: that, in fact, Jesus is the heart
of the gospel.

Others will see the heart of the good news in the way Jesus
directs our attention to the needs of the poor and in God's
continuing concern for the disadvantaged and outcast. For
them, the heart of the gospel is more to do with social action
than with personal salvation.

Neither aspect is actually likely to be seen as exclusive; it is more a matter of emphasis. Each will see in Jesus the key to the good news – what he did and what he said. Without reference to Jesus and what he did, social action can become merely a programme of good works without any specific reference to God. But without the application of faith in concern for social justice, belief in Jesus can become a matter of individual piety.

But if that is the case, what was the good news that Jesus preached during his earthly ministry? He is certainly reported as having told his disciples that he would undergo great suffering, be rejected by the religious authorities, be killed and on the third day be raised (see Luke 9:21-2). The disciples didn't want to face such a possibility, and Peter told Jesus off for saying such things, receiving a rebuke for his pains (Mark 8:31-33). But it was only later, when members of the early Church reflected on all that had happened to Jesus together with their experience of forgiveness and new life found in Jesus, that his death and resurrection were seen as central to the good news that they would proclaim to the world.

Jesus, however, did not preach a gospel so centred upon himself. He was not himself the heart of his good news. Jesus' preaching and teaching were more about the kingdom of God and the forgiving and saving work of God. He may well have seen himself as the agent in bringing that kingdom close, but it was God's action rather than his own that filled his message. Because the early Church was convinced that Jesus was, in fact, key to this action of God, they changed the emphasis and placed Jesus at the heart of the good news of the kingdom and of salvation.

Since the coming of the day of the Lord that Jesus looked for has yet to happen, this aspect of the good news has given way to a much more Jesus-centred gospel in which the cross has been a particular focus. This is interesting when one considers that the first depiction of the cross was, in fact, in a piece of ironic graffiti by a pagan and didn't appear until 300 years after the actual event.

Luke, unlike Matthew and Mark, avoids using the noun (good news) but does use the verb (to tell good news). Originally, the word was used about telling good news of victory, and this, of course, fits well with the interpretation of the cross that sees it as Christ's victory over sin and death. It was this emphasis on the promise of eternal life that so attracted Roman citizens, especially the poor, away from paganism to the new Christian faith. The Roman gods promised victory in battle and expansion of the empire. For the middle class and 'aristocracy', this could mean wealth and status, but it had little general benefit for the poor. The distinctive element of the new Jewish sect centred on Jesus was that it offered a life beyond this, a life where the injustices of this life were made good. Even the brutal suppression of Christians under Diocletian could not stop the spread of Christianity because the threat of death did not outweigh the promise of eternal life.

In the original version of the Isaiah passage that Jesus read in the synagogue at Nazareth, the good news was preached to 'the oppressed' but Luke has changed this to read 'the poor'. He seems to have had a special concern for the poor and the disadvantaged, and he mentions them more than the other Gospels do. He appears to have meant those who were literally poor. In his version of the Beatitudes (Luke 6:20-3) is the straightforward statement, 'Blessed are you who are poor, for yours is the kingdom of God.' By comparison, Matthew says, 'Blessed are the poor in spirit, for theirs is the kingdom of heaven' (Matthew 5:3). In the Psalms, 'the poor' or 'the needy (the word being the same in the Hebrew) can also mean those who are humble (e.g. Psalm 9:18), oppressed (e.g. Psalm 35:10) or weak (e.g. Psalm 72:13).

We see here something of those same twin emphases noted above – on the one hand the spiritual aspect is emphasised; on the other there is social understanding. It is still with us and can be seen either as a theological difference or one of temperament (or perhaps a mixture of both). There are some, notably among the evangelical wing of the Church, who emphasise the fact that a person without Christ is spiritually impoverished and that preaching the good news of Christ's forgiveness and new life is to offer inner riches with eternal significance. Others emphasise the Christian imperative to work for the good of the poor through social action as a way of proclaiming the kingdom value of justice. This apparent divide is, of course, often blurred, and it is noteworthy, for example, that among some young evangelical voters in America, there was support for Barack Obama precisely because of his concern for social justice.

Proclamation is not only a matter of preaching words. It is also action – doing something individually and socially that makes a difference to the lives of the poor. Such action is to make people free, not dependent; to make them more able to make choices and take advantage of opportunities, but not to tie them into a culture of dependency. The importance of freedom is a constant theme in the message of the prophets and is to be understood through a rich diversity of meanings, mundane and spiritual.

Session one

Aim

To consider the biblical understanding of 'the gospel' and 'the poor' and to discuss what proclaiming good news to the poor might mean today.

Music might be played as the group prepares for the session. The first of the Advent candles may be lit. As the candle is lit, 'Kindle a flame' or 'The Lord is my light' might be said or sung.

Prayer

Come Holy Spirit
and open to us the treasures of God's word.
Grant us a readiness to listen
and an openness to learn;
that through the riches of your gifts
we may better understand the needs of the poor
and the good news to be proclaimed.
We ask this in the name of Jesus
who came as a light to the nations. Amen.

Readings

I know that the Lord maintains the cause of the needy,
and executes justice for the poor.

Psalm 140:12

Give the king your justice, O God,
and your righteousness to a king's son.

May he judge your people with righteousness,
and your poor with justice . . .
For he delivers the needy when they call,
the poor and those who have no helper,
he has pity on the weak and the needy,
and saves the lives of the needy.

Psalm 72:1-2, 12-13

Praise the Lord!
Praise, O servants of the Lord;
praise the name of the Lord . . .
Who is like the Lord our God,
who is seated on high,
who looks far down
on the heavens and on the earth?
He raises the poor from the dust,
and lifts the needy from the ash heap,
to make them sit with princes,
with the princes of his people.

Psalm 113:1, 5-8

Those who oppress the poor insult their maker,
but those who are kind to the needy honour him.

Proverbs 14:31

'You always have the poor with you, but you do not
always have me.'

John 12:8

Points for discussion

A. How would you describe the gospel?

- Following the 2011 census it was suggested that poor people are more likely to be religious than the rich. Is the gospel to the poor the same as the gospel to the rich?
- In what ways do you understand the gospel to be a spiritual message, and in what ways is it a social message?
- In what ways does your church seek to 'proclaim the gospel'?

B.

- It is no use preaching to a starving person about his soul before you have fed him.
- A poor person may be poor for a lifetime but his soul is eternal. Feed his soul.
- What truths do you think lie in these contrasting points of view?

C. According to internationally accepted standards, anyone earning less than 60p a day (US $1) is living below the poverty line – i.e. they do not earn enough to live on. In Europe, 3.5 per cent of the population live below the poverty line. In south Asia it is 43.1 per cent.

In the UK, a household is deemed to be in poverty if its income is less than 60 per cent of median (average) household income for the year in question. The value of this poverty line in terms of pounds per week depends on the number of people in the household, reflecting the fact that larger households need more money (although not proportionately more) than smaller ones in order to achieve the same standard of living:

- £124 per week for a single adult
- £210 per week for a lone parent with two children under 14

- £214 per week for a couple with no children
- £300 per week for a couple with two children under 14.

- Do you think there is such a thing as absolute poverty or is it always relative? How do these figures affect the way you might consider the UK's overseas aid programme? Should charity always begin at home?

D. In Luke's Gospel, Jesus is reported as saying, 'Blessed are you who are poor.' In Matthew's Gospel, Jesus is reported as saying: 'Blessed are the poor in spirit.'

- How would you understand the difference?
- In what sense might 'the poor' be happy or blessed?
- Do you think Jesus is referring to now on earth or to the future in heaven?

E. Jesus said, 'You always have the poor with you.' Is poverty inevitable? If it is, is there any point in trying to do something about it?

F. Nearly four million children are living in poverty in the UK (after housing costs).

- The proportion of children living in poverty grew from 1 in 10 in 1979 to 1 in 3 in 1998. In 2012, 30 per cent of children in Britain were living in poverty.
- The UK has one of the worst rates of child poverty in the industrialised world.
- The majority (59 per cent) of poor children live in a household where at least one adult works.
- 40 per cent of poor children live in a household headed by a lone parent. The majority of poor children (57 per cent) live in a household headed by a couple.[1]

---

1. End Child Poverty http://www.endchildpoverty.org.uk/ (accessed 7 May 2013).

- Parents will spend an average of £112.50 on Christmas presents for each of their children, a straw poll has found.[2]

• How do these statistics affect your view of the fact that it is often said that Christmas is a time for children?

Reflection

Spend a few moments in silence reflecting on the discussion.

Members may like to focus their thoughts on the words of one of the hymns given in the Appendix and/or after the silence the group may choose to sing the hymn together.

Prayer

For the riches of God's gifts we give thanks;
for his love and his mercy we give thanks;
for the promise of his Son we give thanks.
For all who live in poverty of possessions we pray to the Father;
for all who live in poverty of spirit we pray to the Father;
for all who proclaim the gospel of hope we pray to the Father.

The Lord's Prayer

We look for the coming of the Lord of light, the Child of Bethlehem, the protector of the poor.

Come, Lord Jesus.

---

2. *Daily Telegraph*, 15 December 2012.

Week two

Release to captives

Introduction

> The spirit of the Lord God is upon me,
> because the Lord has anointed me;
> he has sent me . . .
> to proclaim liberty to the captives,
> and release to the prisoners.
>
> *Isaiah 61:1*

'The Spirit of the Lord is upon me, because he has anointed me to bring good news to the poor.
He has sent me to proclaim release to the captives.'

Luke 4:18

There were two clear marks to the vocation of the prophet – he was anointed and he was sent.

In the case of the king and the high priest, the anointing – the pouring, or smearing, of oil over the head – was done literally, indicating their consecration to their office.

You shall anoint Aaron and his sons, and consecrate them, in order that they may serve as priests.

Exodus 30:30

Samuel took a phial of oil and poured it on [Saul's] head, and kissed him; he said, 'The Lord has anointed you ruler over his people Israel. You shall reign over the people of the Lord and you will save them from the hand of their enemies all around.'

1 Samuel 10:1

In the case of the prophet this was understood in a metaphorical sense – the Lord anointing the prophet by the pouring out of his Spirit upon him. In Isaiah 42:1-7 the Lord declares that he has put his Spirit upon the prophet (anointed him, consecrated him) and sets out the tasks he has been consecrated for.

In the case of Jesus, this anointing with the Spirit is understood by the Gospel writers as having taken place at his baptism.

> Now when all the people were baptised, and when Jesus also had been baptised and was praying, the heaven was opened, and the Holy Spirit descended upon him in bodily form like a dove. And a voice came from heaven, 'You are my Son, the Beloved; with you I am well pleased.'
>
> *Luke 3:21-2 (cf Matthew 3:16-17; Mark 1:9-11;*
> *John 1:29-34; see also Acts 4:27, 10:38)*

Although we often speak of Jesus Christ almost as though these were his forename and surname, more strictly we should speak of Jesus the Christ (or Jesus who is the Christ) – Christ meaning 'the anointed'. It describes his status as the one anointed by God, and his role as the kingly figure who would be his people's saviour. 'Messiah' also means 'anointed' (see Daniel 9:25-6; John 1:41).

As well as the anointing there was the positive 'sending'. Prophets were often reluctant to speak the words they felt they had been given to proclaim. Their message was often hard and unpopular, but they were impelled by their sense of a vocation through which God sent them as messengers, as his voice to his people. They were appointed by God and came, as it were, from the presence of God. We see this in the account of Isaiah's call:

Then I heard the voice of the Lord saying, 'Whom shall I send, and who will go for us?' And I said, 'Here am I; send me!'

Isaiah 6:8

Jeremiah came to understand that he had been consecrated even before he was born and appointed as a prophet to the nations. Yet he felt inadequate to the task:

Then I said 'Ah, Lord God! Truly I do not know how to speak, for I am only a boy.' But the Lord said to me, 'Do not say, "I am only a boy"; for you shall go to all to whom I send you, and you shall speak whatever I command you. Do not be afraid of them, for I am with you to deliver you,' says the Lord.

Jeremiah 1:6-8

Jesus, too, was understood as having been sent by and from God:

But [Jesus] said to them, 'I must proclaim the good news of the kingdom of God to the other cities also; for I was sent for this purpose.'

Luke 4:43

'The works that the Father has given me to complete, the very works that I am doing, testify on my behalf that the Father has sent me.'

John 5:36 (see also John 17:3, 8, 23)

The sending of Jesus can be understood as part of the continuing outgoing activity of God which is at the heart of the nature of God – what has been called the *missio dei*. All mission originates with God – it is his initiative. And just as Jesus was 'sent', so he sent his disciples: 'See, I am sending you out like sheep into the midst of wolves; so be wise as serpents and innocent as doves' (Matthew 10:16; see also Matthew 28:19; John 17:18).

One of the tasks that Isaiah understood he had been anointed for and sent to do was to proclaim liberty and release. Jesus adopted this as one of his tasks.

A distinction can be made between those who are captive and those who are prisoners, although there is inevitably some overlap. In the Old Testament, 'captive' nearly always refers to those who have been captured and taken into exile; this is certainly in the mind of Isaiah as we find it in chapters 40–55 where the setting for the prophecies is the people's exile in Babylon. In older translations such as the King James Bible, the word 'captive' was used, where in more modern translations the term is usually translated as 'exile' or 'taken into exile' – e.g. Jeremiah 24:1, 43:3. We can note, however, that when nations other than the people of God are mentioned, the word captivity occurs more frequently – e.g. 'Woe to you, O Moab! The people of Chemosh have perished, for your sons have been taken captive, and your daughters into captivity' (Jeremiah 48:46).

The passage in Isaiah 61, however, speaks of captives at a time when the exile was over and the people had returned to their homeland. Captivity may therefore have come to be associated with any form of oppression, and we shall be looking at that in more detail in Session 4.

Prisoners may be considered in a more general way – as those who were 'bound' or 'incarcerated'. No distinction is made between those who were imprisoned as the result of an actual or perceived wrongdoing and those who had been imprisoned unjustly or on broadly 'political' grounds. Joseph may have been put in prison on a charge trumped up by Pharaoh's wife, but there is no suggestion that other prisoners, including the chief cup-bearer and chief baker, had been unfairly imprisoned.

Exactly who the 'prisoners' were in Isaiah's prophecy is not exactly clear. Exiles were not normally put in prison so it is unlikely that they are being referred to. In Isaiah 42:6-7 the Lord speaks to his Servant:

I have given you as a covenant to the people, a light to the nations, to open the eyes that are blind, to bring out the prisoners from the dungeon, from the prison those who sit in darkness.

It has been suggested that 'prison' is being used here in a metaphorical sense and refers to the darkness and ignorance in which foreign nations are bound through their paganism. If this is how Jesus (and the Gospel writers) understood such passages, then the release he is referring to is freedom from the grip of sin. However, the story of the imprisonment of the apostles (Acts 5:17-26) and Peter's imprisonment (Acts 12:1-17) indicate that God's power was also understood to extend to those who were literally in prison.

Session two

Aim

To consider how we might view vocation in terms of 'anointing' and 'sending' and the release promised to prisoners.

Music might be played as the group prepares for the session. The second of the Advent candles may be lit. As the candle is lit, 'Kindle a flame' or 'The Lord is my light' might be said or sung.

Prayer

Come Holy Spirit
and open to us the treasures of God's word.
Grant us a readiness to listen
and an openness to learn;
that through your anointing
we may understand our calling
as servants of others,
proclaiming release
to those who are imprisoned.
We ask this in the name of Jesus
who came as a light to the nations. Amen.

Readings

I cry to you, O Lord;
I say, 'You are my refuge,
my portion in the land of the living.'
Give heed to my cry,
for I am brought very low.

Save me from my persecutors,
for they are too strong for me.
Bring me out of prison,
so that I may give thanks to your name.
The righteous will surround me,
for you will deal bountifully with me.

Psalm 142:5-7

Then the king will say to those at his right hand, 'Come, you that are blessed by my Father, inherit the kingdom prepared for you from the foundation of the world; for I was hungry and you gave me food, I was thirsty and you gave me something to drink, I was a stranger and you welcomed me, I was naked and you gave me clothing, I was sick and you took care of me, I was in prison and you visited me.' Then the righteous will answer him, 'Lord when was it that we saw you hungry and gave you food, or thirsty and gave you something to drink? And when was it that we saw you a stranger and welcomed you, or naked and gave you clothing? And when was it that we saw you sick or in prison and visited you?' And the king will answer them, 'Truly I tell you, just as you did it to one of the least of these who are members of my family, you did it to me.'

Matthew 25:34-40

Points for discussion

A. It can be claimed that baptism is the 'anointing' of those called to serve God. It is all the 'authorisation' needed for the Christian to know that he/she is called, commissioned and sent to witness to God's love in Christ and proclaim the gospel.

35

- How far would you view baptism in this way? In what ways do you believe that vocation has more specific meanings?

B. It is seldom that people these days are taken captive into exile, but many find themselves driven from their homeland.

- In 2011 the United Nations Refugee Agency reported that for the fifth consecutive year the number of forcibly displaced people worldwide exceeded 42 million. This figure included internally displaced people, asylum seekers and refugees.

- In December 2012 this report was issued on the Refugee International website:

  The civil war in Syria has forced large numbers of Syrians from their homes, and in many cases from the country entirely. Refugees continue to flee in record numbers, and there are currently almost 400,000 registered or waiting for registration in Iraq, Jordan, Lebanon, and Turkey combined. The United Nations has said it expects this number could reach 700,000 by 31 December, 2012. About half of all the registered Syrians are living in camps, but the other half remain in local host communities trying to get by on their own.[3]

- In the UK, asylum seekers remains a sensitive political issue.

- Discuss what it would feel like to be forced from your home and your country, taking with you only the possessions you could carry.

---

3. www.refugeesinternational.org (accessed 12 May 2013).

C. England and Wales has one of the highest rates of incarceration in Western Europe. In 2012, an average of 148 people in every 100,000 were in prison, cf 94 in Germany and 85 in France. In November 2012, the prison population in England and Scotland was 86,047.

- As a Christian, what view do you take of these statistics? How far is prison the most appropriate way of dealing with criminal behaviour?

D. What experience, if any, have members of the group of visiting a prison? How far does it agree with the picture given by some newspapers that prison is like a glorified Butlins?

E. How might the group encourage the local church to take seriously Jesus' words about visiting prisoners?

F. On release from prison, an ex-offender is given £46. How would you seek to build a new life with that amount?

G. It is sometimes suggested that the Church only increases people's sense of guilt, yet Jesus promises to release us from the imprisonment of guilt and sin. How do we experience that freedom, and how as individuals and as a local church do we make that available to others?

H. Freedom is a gift that enriches our lives; freedom is a gift that calls us to responsibility; freedom is a gift that too often is turned into licence.

Reflection

Spend a few moments in silence reflecting on the discussion.

Members may like to focus their thoughts on the words of one of the hymns given in the Appendix and/or after the silence the group may choose to sing the hymn together.

Prayer

For the forgiveness of sins, we give thanks;
for release from guilt, we give thanks;
for the freedoms we enjoy, we give thanks.
For all who live in exile from their homes, we pray to
the Father;
for all who are in prison, we pray to the Father;
for all who work to bring liberty of spirit, we pray to
the Father.

The Lord's Prayer

We look for the coming of the Lord of light, the Child of Bethlehem, the giver of freedom.

Come, Lord Jesus.

Sight to the blind

Introduction

> I am the Lord, I have called you in righteousness,
> I have taken you by the hand and kept you;
> I have given you as a covenant to the people,
> a light to the nations,
> to open the eyes that are blind.
>
> *Isaiah 42:6-7*

'The Spirit of the Lord is upon me, because he has anointed me to bring good news to the poor.
He has sent me to proclaim release to the captives, and recovery of sight to the blind.'

Luke 4:17

By the age of 46, John Milton was completely blind. It is generally agreed that it was around this time that he wrote the poem 'On his blindness', in which he sought to come to terms with his blindness and the demands of God. He concluded that while many rush all over the world to serve God, 'They also serve who only stand and wait.' His most famous poems, 'Paradise Lost' and 'Paradise Regained', were written in his blindness and at a time when he was impoverished.

Milton certainly suffered as a result of his blindness, but he found a way both of coping with it and of not allowing it to prevent his work as a poet. Not everyone has that opportunity, nor what he called 'patience', and blindness can be devastating. Statistically, blindness or serious sight impairment increasingly affects people in their later years.

In the UK, one in nine of those over the age of 60 are currently living with sight loss, and by 2050 the total number of people with sight loss is expected to reach four million. This is a serious figure, not least when it is estimated that 50 per cent of sight loss can be avoided.

In developing countries the statistics are far, far worse, and the social and economic effects of blindness are also proportionately more severe. Of the 285 million people globally suffering from sight impairment, 90 per cent live in the developing world.

In times of less advanced medical help and when the causes of blindness were less known and less treatable, blindness was a serious problem. Little wonder that it was among the social and personal ills that Isaiah saw that the Lord had called his people to rectify. In his account of the event at the Nazareth synagogue, Luke inserted the recovery of sight to the blind into the list of tasks that the 'anointed one' was to fulfil as outlined in the prophecy of Isaiah in chapter 61. Later in his Gospel, Luke gave accounts of Jesus indeed curing the blind (Luke 18:35-43; see also Mark 8:11-26).

In the light of these accounts it is likely that Luke and the other Gospel writers saw blindness and its cure in realistic, though miraculous, terms. In Mark's understanding it was one of the manifestations of evil against which Jesus battled. But both Luke and Mark understood blindness in spiritual as well as simply physical terms. The context of both the healing of the blind man at Bethsaida (Mark) and of the man at Jericho (Luke) indicates that both Mark and Luke understood physical blindness as a metaphor of a failure to understand on the part of either the Jewish religious leaders or the disciples.

The crowds had come out to listen to Jesus' teaching. Realising that they had come without any food, Jesus instructed his disciples to collect what they could. From seven loaves and a few small fish, he provided enough for the crowd of 4000. This aroused the attention of some Pharisees and they engaged Jesus in discussion, asking him for a sign as evidence of his authority.

In Mark's account, Jesus refuses to give them a sign, and he gets in a boat to cross to the other side of the lake. While making the crossing, he warns the disciples about the 'yeast of the Pharisees' – a saying that confuses the disciples, who think he is referring to the miraculous feeding they have just witnessed. Jesus remonstrates with them: 'Do you still not perceive or understand?' he asks. 'Are your hearts hardened? Do you have eyes, and fail to see?' He reminds them of the number of loaves they had and the number of basketfuls of scraps they gathered up. The seven and the twelve were obviously significant, but the disciples still did not understand.

They arrive at Bethsaida and a blind man is brought to Jesus. His friends beg Jesus to heal him. Jesus 'anoints' his eyes with mud and spittle and at first the man sees men looking like trees walking about. After a second 'anointing', he sees everything clearly. Gaining sight can be a gradual process; so, too, is gaining insight (Mark 8:11-26).

If the blindness of the religious leaders was their failure to realise the significance of Jesus as the 'anointed prophet', the disciples' failure was more specific: they could not see that the only way he would be able to fulfil his divine commission would be through suffering, death and resurrection. When, according to Luke, he told them he would be mocked, maltreated, flogged and killed, 'they understood nothing about all these things; in fact, what he said was hidden from them.'

As they continued their journey to Jerusalem, they came to Jericho where a blind man sat at the roadside, begging. He addressed Jesus as the Son of David and asked him to have pity and to restore his sight. Jesus did no more than tell him, 'Receive your sight,' and he was immediately cured. The Word was sufficient to bring sight, to give insight (Luke 18:31-43; see also Matthew 20:17-34; John 8:30–9:12).

Metaphors drawn from blindness or sight impairment do not only occur in religious texts. They are found in everyday conversation. We talk of going down 'blind alleys' when a path of action leads nowhere. A 'blind date' brings two people together who have never met before. A 'blind plant' is one that produces no flower. People who not only fail to see the truth that is being presented to them but constantly refuse to do so are characterised as 'none so blind as those who won't see.' In the 1962 song 'Blowin' in the wind'. Bob Dylan asks the questions, 'How many times must a man look up before he can see the sky? How many times can a man turn his head and pretend that he just doesn't see?'

Jesus warned his followers that it is vital to ensure that the truth – the 'light' – that guides their lives is truly light and not darkness:

> Your eye is the lamp of your body. If your eye is healthy, your whole body is full of light; but if it is not healthy, your body is full of darkness. Therefore consider whether the light in you is not darkness. If then your whole body is full of light, with no part of it in darkness, it will be as full of light as when a lamp gives you light with its rays.
>
> *Luke 11:34-6*

The use of blindness as a metaphor for failing or refusing to see truth has led some blind people to feel that this can lead to a subtle, even subconscious, form of discrimination or prejudice by which people make assumptions that blind people are in some sense less able or intelligent. However, not all metaphors from blindness have negative connotations. We speak approvingly of 'blind justice' in the belief that judgements made purely on the basis of appearances can offer poor justice. This reminds us that people spoke approvingly of the fact that Jesus knew what was in a person's heart and did not judge by appearances. 'Blind trust' is more ambiguous.

Kittens and puppies are born blind (and deaf) as this protects their developing optical systems both from damaging particles and the bright light that could damage their delicate photosensitive receptors. The fanatical Saul was blind for a period after his challenging and life-changing experience on the road to Damascus. At one level, this might be understood as a result of the bright light that confronted him, but at another, the blindness represented the period of transition from one set of convictions to another, from one way of seeing the world to another. His 'healing' through Ananias after a period of three days was followed by his baptism. 'And immediately something like scales fell from his eyes, and his sight was restored. Then he got up and was baptised, and after taking some food, he regained his strength (Acts 9:1-19). The response to a sudden revelation has often been described in a similar way.

Session three

Aim

To understand something of the nature of both physical and spiritual blindness and the help that may be given to those who are blind.

Music might be played as the group prepares for the session. The third of the Advent candles may be lit. As the candle is lit, 'Kindle a flame' or 'The Lord is my light' might be said or sung.

Prayer

Come Holy Spirit
and open to us the treasures of God's word.
Grant us a readiness to listen
and an openness to learn;
that through your anointing
we may receive the gift of insight,
that we might live by the light of your truth.
We pray for all whose sight is impaired,
at birth or through accident, disease and old age;
and we pray for all who work to help them.
We ask this in the name of Jesus
who came as a light to the nations. Amen.

Readings

The law of the Lord is perfect,
reviving the soul;

the decrees of the Lord are sure,
making wise the simple;
the precepts of the Lord are right,
rejoicing the heart;
the commandment of the Lord is clear,
enlightening the eyes;
the fear of the Lord is pure,
enduring for ever;
the ordinances of the Lord are true
and righteous altogether.

Psalm 19:7-9

They were on the road, going up to Jerusalem, and Jesus was walking ahead of them; they were amazed, and those who followed were afraid. He took the twelve aside again and began to tell them what was to happen to him, saying, 'See, we are going up to Jerusalem, and the Son of Man will be handed over to the chief priests and the scribes, and they will condemn him to death; then they will hand him over to the Gentiles; they will mock him, and spit upon him, and flog him, and kill him; and after three days he will rise again.'

James and John, the sons of Zebedee, came forward to him and said to him, 'Teacher, we want you to do for us whatever we ask of you.' And he said to them, 'What is it you want me to do for you?' And they said to him, 'Grant us to sit, one at your right hand and one at your left, in your glory.' But Jesus said to them, 'You do not know what you are asking. Are you able to drink the cup that I drink, or be baptised with the baptism that I am baptised with?' They replied, 'We are able.' Then Jesus said to them, 'The cup that I drink you will drink;

and with the baptism with which I am baptised, you will be baptised; but to sit at my right hand or at my left is not mine to grant, but it is for those for whom it has been prepared.'

When the ten heard this, they began to be angry with James and John. So Jesus called them and said to them, 'You know that among the Gentiles those whom they recognise as their rulers lord it over them, and their great ones are tyrants over them. But it is not so among you; but whoever wishes to become great among you must be your servant, and whoever wishes to be first among you must be slave of all. For the Son of Man came not to be served but to serve, and to give his life a ransom for many.'

They came to Jericho. As he and his disciples and a large crowd were leaving Jericho, Bartimaeus son of Timaeus, a blind beggar, was sitting by the roadside. When he heard that it was Jesus of Nazareth, he began to shout out and say, 'Jesus, Son of David, have mercy on me!' Many sternly ordered him to be quiet, but he cried out even more loudly, 'Son of David, have mercy on me!' Jesus stood still and said, 'Call him here.' And they called the blind man, saying to him, 'Take heart; get up, he is calling you.' So throwing off his cloak, he sprang up and came to Jesus. Then Jesus said to him, 'What do you want me to do for you?' The blind man said to him, 'My teacher, let me see again.' Jesus said to him, 'Go; your faith has made you well.' Immediately he regained his sight and followed him on the way.

Mark 10:32-52

Points for discussion

A. In what ways did the disciples display their 'blindness' in the passage just read? What did it take for them to gain insight?

B. Discuss what differences it would have made in coming to this meeting had you been blind.

C. Jesus asked, 'Can a blind person guide a blind person? Will not both fall into a pit?' (Luke 6:39). What do you understand by this saying, and what does it imply for a church congregation?

D.

- There are almost two million people in the UK who are living with sight loss that has a significant impact on their daily lives.
- There are 40,000 blind and partially sighted children and young people in the UK.
- One in every nine people aged over 60 is currently living with sight loss.
- Well over two-fifths of blind and partially sighted people feel 'moderately' or 'completely' cut off from people and things around them.[4]

- What could a local church do to help those living locally who are partially sighted and who feel 'moderately' or 'completely' cut off from people and things around them?

E. Share with members of the group any experience you have had of 'scales falling' from your eyes.

---

4. Action for blind people, www. fightforsight.org.uk (accessed 12 May 2013).

F. How do you respond to the suggestion that the stories of the healing of blind people and the way lack of sight is treated in the New Testament encourage people to have a false idea of blind people?

G. John Newton, the slave trader, radically changed his views on the slave trade. He wrote the hymn 'Amazing Grace', of which the first verse is:

> Amazing grace, how sweet the sound
> that saved a wretch like me.
> I once was lost but now am found,
> was blind, but now I see.

Discuss other examples of major shifts in public and social views or attitudes. What current attitudes would you like to see changed?

Reflection

Spend a few moments in silence reflecting on the discussion.

Members may like to focus their thoughts on the words of one of the hymns given in the Appendix and/or after the silence the group may choose to sing the hymn together.

Prayer

To keep us from false teaching and misunderstandings,
may your light surround us.
To lead us in the way of your truth,
may your light surround us.
To fill us with understanding for those whose sight is impaired,
may your light surround us.

To overcome the darkness of our fears,
may your light surround us.
To bring us hope in times of doubt,
may your light surround us.

The Lord's Prayer

We look for the coming of the Lord of light, the Child of Bethlehem, the giver of freedom.

Come, Lord Jesus.

Week four

Freedom to the oppressed

Introduction

> Is not this the fast that I choose:
> to loose the bonds of injustice,
> to undo the thongs of the yoke,
> to let the oppressed go free,
> and to break every yoke?
> Is it not to share your bread with the hungry,
> and bring the homeless poor into your house;
> when you see the naked, to cover them,
> and not to hide yourself from your own kin?
>
> *Isaiah 58:6-7*

'The Spirit of the Lord is upon me, because he has anointed me to bring good news to the poor.
He has sent me to proclaim release to the captives, and recovery of sight to the blind, to let the oppressed go free.'

Luke 4:18

The literal meaning of the phrase translated 'let the oppressed go free' is 'to send away in freedom those who have been broken in pieces.' As a metaphor, it is powerful but not entirely logical, as it does not make explicit that those broken should first be mended. It does, however, have a dramatic and dynamic quality that is perhaps lacking in the associations with oppression.

Oppression speaks more of a heavy burden weighing down the victim, a burden that has to be carried while the normal

51

act of living goes on. It is restrictive and, to those who are oppressed, the promise of freedom would certainly be a welcome release.

Oppression is a chronic, long-term condition, and in the struggles for power and empire there have always been those who have suffered oppression. It was true in Isaiah's time, in the days of Jesus and is still true today. Slavery is perhaps its most obvious general manifestation, where entire races are subjected to a state of oppression and where there is little hope of freedom.

Exile has its own characteristics, and those who are driven from their own country as refugees are oppressed by their loss, even if attempts are made to alleviate their desperate state. For others, oppression can arise simply as a result of their gender, their colour, their race, their sexual orientation or their economic condition.

Human society, no matter how apparently enlightened, too often treats some of its members in ways that are experienced as oppression. The Declaration of Human Rights has provided nations with a yardstick by which to measure how well they behave towards their citizens, but a declaration is not enough. There is a constant need for human rights to be monitored and for pressure to be brought upon those who are failing to promote such rights.

Oppression is not simply a passive withdrawal of people's rights; it is the active constraining of their freedoms. This is what is conveyed by the image of the yoke. The oxen have no right to decide which way to turn but must follow the direction of the driver exerting pressure through the yoke. It is both a weight and a means of limiting freedom of choice. To be released from that is to enjoy a greater physical freedom and, metaphorically, a greater moral and spiritual freedom as well. That a yoke ensures that a task may be fulfilled does not alter the fact that it also restricts.

Right up until the middle of the last century, yokes could be seen being used by farmers carrying pails of milk from the cowsheds, or taking buckets of feed to their stock. The yoke helped to distribute the weight of the load across the shoulders, but the wearer had little freedom to do much else. A yoke has the power to limit a person to a functional task – and people are more than that. This is why it can convey the notion of oppression – for an individual as well as for large groups of people, or even for a whole nation.

Paradoxically, when Jesus promised that he would offer rest to those coming to him who are weary and carrying heavy burdens, he did so by inviting them to take on his yoke – 'For my yoke is easy, and my burden is light' (Matthew 11:28-30). To be directed by Jesus is to discover our true selves and therefore the freedom to be ourselves. Saint Augustine reflected this in his prayer: 'Grant us so to know thee that we may truly love thee, and so to love thee that we may fully serve thee, whom to serve is perfect freedom.'[5]

Poverty is a kind of oppression and restriction in itself. It is not simply that it limits choices and the ability to purchase things, but it is also oppressive in that there often appears to be no way out from under its burden. It weighs heavily upon the human spirit; it depresses. At its most severe it means that there is nothing else a person can do but put all their energies into survival. And that is not what we mean by living, nor by freedom.

Oppression can be the result of the actions of others. It can result from the conditions of one's environment.

---

5. Frank Colquhoun (ed), Prayer 1592 in *Parish Prayers*, where it is given as 'after St Augustine', (Hodder and Stoughton, 1967).

Long-term drought produces the oppression of famine. But the constant fear of flooding can also feel oppressive – as people in the west of England experienced in the repeated floods of 2012. Hopefully this was a temporary 'oppression', although the uncertainties of climate change bring their own kind of anxious weight for many people, not least those living in low-lying regions.

There is also oppression that arises from within oneself – the oppression of obsession or addiction, the oppression of guilt and anxiety. These can be debilitating, restricting and a burden from which the sufferer longs to be free.

The effect of a more immediate, dramatic event can feel less often like oppression and more like being broken into pieces. The experience is reflected in the way it is described. People say, for example, 'I was shattered.' We speak of being 'broken-hearted' and of 'just going to pieces.' Our worlds can 'fall apart' and our dreams end up 'in tatters'. All of these speak of a loss of the wholeness we had experienced or had hoped for. What had appeared to fit well together is wrenched apart. The unity is broken, the harmony disturbed.

This is in many ways a description of the world of human relationships, for all that it is also loving and creative. Things jar and split apart. There are broken relationships at the personal level and alienation in society and between nations. Secular explanations for this condition would no doubt look to such things as the fight for resources and the struggle for power, each rooted in our genetic make-up and surviving primal instincts. The person of religion looks into the heart and the spirit.

In the Jewish/Christian tradition is the story of the brokenness that came about through disobedience and which is described in the story of Adam and Eve. Other faiths have their own stories and myths that seek to cast light on the mystery of our human brokenness. The Christian faith may have sometimes overemphasised the wickedness of humanity, but it has never hidden from its reality. The hope of freedom from such brokenness is, for the Christian, not to be found in greater moral endeavour, nor in reforming programmes and renewed structures, necessary and helpful though these may be, but in the transformation of the human heart through the forgiveness, grace and empowering of God.

Nevertheless, where oppression and brokenness can be seen as the result of human activity, either by individuals or institutions, freedom may also be brought about by human endeavour. There are peacemakers, and those who work for the reinstatement of refugees. Groups seek to monitor human rights and to bring about change where those rights are abused. Agencies seek to relieve famine and to develop local resources. But such moves towards restoration and renewal only come about because there is a desire, a will, to find the possibility of new wholeness and transforming freedom. Such a will, such action, arises from hearts that are themselves more in harmony with the wholeness that God seeks and enables, whether or not he is recognised.

At the international level, it was the threat of war and the subsequent experience of exile that was experienced by the Jews of Isaiah's time as oppression and brokenness. But internally there had already been the oppression of injustice and the burden of deprivation, made worse by a lack of compassion in society. It was against this that prophets like Amos (see Amos 5:21-4) and Isaiah of Jerusalem had spoken, and it was a message taken up by Jesus in the parable of the sheep and the goats (Matthew 25:31-46). Those who are people of the kingdom, who have, as it were, placed themselves under the rule of God's way of justice and love, are the ones who show compassion to the needy. Those whose lives are governed by self-concern and an indifference to justice are those whom Jesus believed were far from the kingdom.

Some have seen Jesus' message of forgiveness as a spiritual understanding of 'freeing the oppressed'. As far as the Gospel writers are concerned, it was in his healing and ministry of exorcism that they saw the oppressed being freed, the broken made whole. An example of this is found in the account in Luke's Gospel of the woman who had been crippled for 18 years. In curing her, Jesus declares, 'Woman, you are set free from your ailment.' Later he asks the Pharisees, who objected to her being cured on the Sabbath, 'Ought not this woman, a daughter of Abraham whom Satan bound for eighteen long years, be set free from this bondage on the sabbath day?' (Luke 13:10-17). So Luke may well have understood this healing as an exorcism.

At a personal and interpersonal level, at a national and a global level, experience forces us to admit to the brokenness of human relationships and that oppression is a present reality, not simply a historical aberration. Both are part of the darkness that the light of the world came to dispel.

Session four

Aim

To understand something of the nature of oppression, both individually and more widely, and the resources of forgiveness and grace that can bring release.

Music might be played as the group prepares for the session. The fourth of the Advent candles may be lit. As the candle is lit, 'Kindle a flame' or 'The Lord is my light' might be said or sung.

Prayer

Come Holy Spirit
and open to us the treasures of God's word.
Grant us a readiness to listen
and an openness to learn;
that through your anointing
we may receive the gift of insight,
that we might live by the light of your truth.
We pray for all whose lives are blighted by oppression;
for those who suffer from broken relationships
and from brokenness of spirit.
Grant them the freedom of your releasing and healing power.
We ask this in the name of Jesus
who came as a light to the nations. Amen.

Readings

The Lord is a stronghold for the oppressed,
a stronghold in times of trouble.

And those who know your name put their trust in you,
for you, O Lord, have not forsaken those who seek you.

Psalm 9:9-10

Now he was teaching in one of the synagogues on the sabbath. And just then there appeared a woman with a spirit that had crippled her for eighteen years. She was bent over and was quite unable to stand up straight. When Jesus saw her, he called her over and said, 'Woman, you are set free from your ailment.' When he laid his hands on her, immediately she stood up straight and began praising God. But the leader of the synagogue, indignant because Jesus had cured on the sabbath, kept saying to the crowd, 'There are six days on which work ought to be done; come on those days and be cured, and not on the sabbath day.' But the Lord answered him and said, 'You hypocrites! Does not each of you on the sabbath untie his ox or his donkey from the manger, and lead it away to give it water? And ought not this woman, a daughter of Abraham whom Satan bound for eighteen long years, be set free from this bondage on the sabbath day?' When he said this, all his opponents were put to shame; and the entire crowd was rejoicing at all the wonderful things that he was doing.

Luke 13:10-17

Points for discussion

A. In what ways do you understand Jesus' saying, 'my yoke is easy' (Matthew 11:30)? How might his 'yoke' bring rest and release from burdens?

B. At the end of 2012 and into 2013 there were large protests in India as a result of the gang rape and murder of a young medical student. The oppression of women in India was highlighted.

- Which groups in England do you think experience oppression, and what might be done about it?

C. On 7 January 2013, John Bingham, Religious Affairs Correspondent for the *Telegraph*, reported on the Pope's New Year message:

> Far from protecting hard-fought freedoms, modern human rights culture is being used to suppress liberty of conscience and restrain Christianity, he said.
>
> In one of his biggest addresses of the year, Benedict XVI said a false concept of human rights had gripped the western world. As a result, he said, religion is being marginalised and symbols of faith, such as the cross, are being treated with growing hostility.

- How far do you think that this is a fair assessment of the position of human rights in the western world?

D. 'Better to light a candle than to curse the darkness.'[6]

- In what ways does/might your church/group seek to 'light a candle' for those who experience oppression?

E. What experience have you had of being weighed down by a burden or being 'broken in pieces'? What helped to relieve the situation, bringing release and healing?

---

6. English proverb. Peter Benenson, founder of Amnesty International, used it at a Human Rights Day Celebration on 10 December 1961.

F. In Greek, the words 'wholeness', 'healing', 'salvation' have linguistic connections. In what ways does this help our understanding of what 'salvation' means?

G. Amos suggested that God is more concerned about justice for the oppressed than religious practices (see Amos 5:21-4). Jesus appears to have felt that releasing an 'oppressed' woman was more important than sticking to the rules about the sabbath.

- In what ways might we today experience a tension between practical compassion and justice, and the demands of religion?

Reflection

Spend a few moments in silence reflecting on the discussion.

Members may like to focus their thoughts on the words of one of the hymns given in the Appendix and/or after the silence the group may choose to sing the hymn together.

Prayer

Come, Lord Jesus, with your healing power
and mend the broken fragments of our fractured world:
the peace between nations torn by violence;
the rights of individuals denied by oppression;
the love between people destroyed by selfishness;
the wholeness of spirit disrupted through sin.
Help us to remove the burden of oppression from others
and to take on your yoke to direct our lives
and to give rest to our souls.
Amen.

The Lord's Prayer

We look for the coming of the Lord of light, the Child of Bethlehem, the giver of freedom.

Come, Lord Jesus.

Week five

The year of the Lord's favour

Introduction

> Thus says the Lord:
> In a time of favour I have answered you,
> on a day of salvation I have helped you;
> I have kept you and given you
> as a covenant to the people,
> to establish the land,
> to apportion the desolate heritages;
> saying to the prisoners, 'Come out',
> to those who are in darkness 'Show yourselves.'
>
> *Isaiah 49:8-9*

> 'The Spirit of the Lord is upon me, because he has anointed me to bring good news to the poor.
> He has sent me to proclaim release to the captives, and recovery of sight to the blind, to let the oppressed go free, to proclaim the year of the Lord's favour.'
>
> *Luke 4:18-19*

The background to the idea of 'the year of the Lord's favour' is to be found in the Old Testament concept of Sabbath and Jubilee. What Jesus was doing in the synagogue was making a royal proclamation of God's Year of Jubilee, which at his baptism and by the anointing of the Spirit he had been commissioned to bring in.

In the Genesis story of creation, God rested on the seventh day (Genesis 2:2). This was the reason for the Jewish tradition, laid down in law, to keep the seventh day holy, as a day of rest (Exodus 20:8-11). But it was not only the people who were to have a rest. The land, too, was to have its sabbath – the sabbatical rest in the seventh year when it was to be left fallow.

The culmination of this came in the fiftieth year – the year of Jubilee. It was a year of release – the land was not ploughed, property reverted to its original owner, debts were remitted, and enslaved Hebrews were to be given their freedom.

> And you shall hallow the fiftieth year and you shall proclaim liberty throughout the land to all its inhabitants. It shall be a jubilee for you: you shall return, every one of you, to your property, and every one of you to your family.
>
> *Leviticus 25:10*

It was a time of rejoicing and thanksgiving, but also a time for strengthening faith in the God who would provide. How far the Jubilee principle was ever put consistently into practice is unclear, but it remained a powerful concept and became an image of the redemptive action of God. It was used by the prophets to announce a time of God's saving activity, and it became the way of speaking about God's final action at the end of time. Release from all kinds of oppression and from darkness are a constant theme. In the bad times it was a word of hope promising freedom and light.

No wonder Luke saw in this phrase from the Isaiah prophecy the heart of the good news that Jesus would preach and enact: Christ, the bringer of freedom and light. It is a very positive way of understanding the whole work and mission of Jesus which is set out in the rest of Luke's Gospel.

But Luke has cut the Isaiah passage short. Isaiah 61:2 proclaims not only the year of the Lord's favour but also 'the day of vengeance of our God.' It would seem that Luke wanted to emphasise the gracious activity of God (and Jesus) and avoid reference to the subject of divine judgement. To some extent, this might be said to reflect the thrust of Jesus' own preaching when compared with that of John the Baptist. In his declaration of the imminent activity of God, John had spoken fiercely about the judgement that would fall on those who failed to repent and be cleansed through baptism (Luke 3:7-14). Jesus was seen to preach more about forgiveness and God's mercy. However, this distinction should not be exaggerated. In the Old and New Testaments the 'time of favour' is constantly set alongside the 'day of vengeance'.

Even a fleeting run through the pages of history reveals that life for individuals and for nations is not, and never has been, plain sailing, a steady journey, a level path. There are storms as well as calms, there are hazards as well as wonders, there are downs as well as ups. Fortunes rise and fall, empires come and go. From a biblical point of view, this is not a matter of chance or some natural rhythm in the sequence of events. In a world in which God is involved, such things reflect the state of the relationship between humanity and God, and especially the relationship between the people of God and their Lord.

But it is not a simple matter of 'ledger keeping' – be good and you will be rewarded; be disobedient and you will be punished. It can certainly look like that at times, but it was more spiritually sophisticated than that in reality, as we can see from the fundamental basis of that relationship between God and his people – the covenant. There are, of course, many covenants in the biblical record – covenants to Noah, to Abraham, to Moses, the new covenant in Jesus. They are sometimes mistakenly described as agreements – if by that we mean a negotiated contract between two parties of equal standing.

All covenants begin and are grounded in the graciousness of God. It is his offer, his promise, which underpins the covenant and to which the people are invited to respond. The two parties are not equal. The promise is that he will be their God and they will be his people; as he is holy they are called also to be holy. This is the language of relationship, of loyalty, trust and response.

The connection of covenant with law that is associated with Moses has tended to overemphasise the concept of command and obedience. For the people who were faithful to the call to be holy, to be the people of this God living in this God's way, there was the promise of blessing. Breaking that relationship through unfaithfulness and a lack of trust meant not only a withdrawal of blessing but also punishment. Without that possibility of 'judgement', the covenant relationship would have had no significance – it would just reflect the way things happen to be and life would carry on regardless.

So there was always the possibility that the 'day of the Lord' would be a day of favour, but there was equally the possibility that it would be a day of vengeance. And the people did not always read the signs right. That was what the prophets were there to do. So Amos (Amos 5:18-20) could say this:

> Alas for you who desire the day of the Lord!
> Why do you want the day of the Lord?
> It is darkness, not light . . .

Is not the day of the Lord darkness, not light,
and gloom with no brightness in it?

But he could also say (Amos 9:13-14):

The time is surely coming, says the Lord,
when the one who ploughs shall overtake the one
who reaps,
and the trader of grapes the one who sows the seed;
the mountains shall drip sweet wine,
and the hills shall flow with it.
I will restore the fortunes of my people Israel,
and they shall rebuild the ruined cities and inhabit them.

For those who want a simplistic picture of God as either a God of judgement or a God of mercy, the biblical picture is confusing for it shows a God who is both. In New Testament terms, what draws these two together and keeps them in a proper relationship is the insistence that God is a God of love with a love that is both holy and gracious, demanding and comforting, punishing and forgiving. The cost of the tension that that entails is borne by God, not us – that is what the cross and resurrection reveal to us.

And that is the good news proclaimed by the one anointed by the Spirit, who is the 'light to the nations'. It is good news for all; it is light for all. It is why a time of Jubilee, a time of God's favour, can be announced with a trumpet sound, for it is a time of release and rejoicing, a time of thanksgiving and the renewal of faith. It is a time inaugurated by the coming of Jesus, a time whose promises and possibilities he has already made possible through his death and resurrection and through the gift of the Spirit. It is a time to be fulfilled at the end of time when he will come again.

The Advent season is a time of hope and of light, of good news and celebration. But these only have depth and value if we also acknowledge all that is oppressive and all that is dark. The coming of Christ as a baby at Bethlehem is the coming of the light that will dispel the darkness and make it possible for us to live as children of the light, playing our part in bringing freedom and light to the places of our world where there is oppression and darkness. The coming of Jesus at the fullness of time is the promise that the light will prevail, that hope is not false, that the promises of a gracious, forgiving, loving God will be fulfilled.

Session five

Preparation

Each person is asked to bring a recent daily newspaper with them.

Aim

To explore the nature of God's gracious action in the coming of Christ and the relation between mercy and judgement in his love for all people.

Music might be played as the group prepares for the session. The fifth of the Advent candles may be lit. As the candle is lit, 'Kindle a flame' or 'The Lord is my light' might be said or sung.

Prayer

Come Holy Spirit
and open to us the treasures of God's word.
Grant us a readiness to listen
and an openness to learn;
that through your anointing
we may rejoice in the Father's goodness towards us,
giving thanks for the coming of Christ
and repenting of all that disrupts our relationship with God.
We ask this in the name of Jesus
who came as a light to the nations. Amen.

Reading

[Jesus said,] 'For God so loved the world that he gave his only Son, so that everyone who believes in him may not perish but may have eternal life.

'Indeed, God did not send the Son into the world to condemn the world, but in order that the world might be saved through him. Those who believe in him are not condemned; but those who do not believe are condemned already, because they have not believed in the name of the only Son of God. And this is the judgement, that the light has come into the world, and people loved darkness rather than light because their deeds were evil. For all who do evil hate the light and do not come to the light, so that their deeds may not be exposed. But those who do what is true come to the light, so that it may be clearly seen that their deeds have been done in God.'

John 3:16-21

Points for discussion

A. What ways do you feel are appropriate for marking Sunday as a 'day of rest' – for individuals and for society as a whole?

B. What event for yourself, or more widely, do you see as a sign of God's 'favour'? In what way would you wish to celebrate it?

C. How would you describe the key characteristics of a good relationship? Are these different to the way you would describe a relationship with God?

D. In pairs, look through a copy of a recent newspaper and identify stories that reflect the 'darkness' of the world and those that reflect the presence of 'light'. Do a quick calculation to discover whether 'dark' stories or 'light' stories predominate. What do you think this says about i) newspapers, and ii) our world?

E. If God is a God of love, how do you understand his judgement and his mercy?

F. In what ways do you believe that the coming of Christ has brought light into the world?

Reflection

Spend a few moments in silence reflecting on the discussion.

Members may like to focus their thoughts on the words of one of the hymns given in the Appendix and/or after the silence the group may choose to sing the hymn together.

Prayer

Almighty God,
in your love, look with mercy
on all that is wrong in our lives and our world;
help us to reject the darkness and to live in your light,
that we may rejoice in the coming of your Son
who is the light of the world, the light to the nations.
In your love, root out what is evil,
in your holiness, strengthen all that is good,
that we may give thanks for your merciful judgement
and celebrate the wonder of your love.
In Jesus Christ's name. Amen.

The Lord's Prayer

We look for the coming of the Lord of light, the Child of Bethlehem, the giver of freedom.

Come, Lord Jesus.

Postscript

Arise, shine; for your light has come,
and the glory of the Lord has risen upon you.
For darkness shall cover the earth,
and thick darkness the peoples;
but the Lord will arise upon you,
and his glory will appear over you.
Nations shall come to your light,
and kings to the brightness of your dawn . . .
Your gates shall always be open;
day and night they shall not be shut,
so that nations shall bring you their wealth,
with their kings led in procession . . .
Violence shall no more be heard in your land,
devastation or destruction within your borders;
you shall call your walls Salvation,
and your gates Praise.
The sun shall no longer be
your light by day,
nor for brightness shall the moon
give light to you by night;
but the Lord will be your everlasting light,
and your God will be your glory.

Isaiah 60:1-3, 11, 18-19

Appendix

Suggested hymns

All of the hymns listed below may be found in *Anglican Hymns Old & New* (Kevin Mayhew, 2008).

Amazing grace, how sweet the sound

Awake, awake: fling off the night!

Christ is the world's Light, he and none other

Christ whose glory fills the skies

Come thou long-expected Jesus

For the healing of the nations

God is love: let heaven adore him

God of mercy, God of grace

Great is the darkness that covers the earth

Hail to the Lord's anointed

Hark, my soul, it is the Lord

Hark the glad sound! The Saviour comes

Heaven shall not wait

Here in this place new light is streaming

I heard the voice of Jesus say

Join the song of praise and protest

Judge eternal, throned in splendour

Kindle a flame

Light of the world

Longing for light, we wait in darkness

Lord, the light of your love is shining

Make way, make way

O come, O come Emmanuel

O day of God, draw nigh

The Lord is my light, my light and salvation

The people that in darkness sat

The Saviour will come

The Spirit lives to set us free

Thou whose almighty word

Waken, O sleeper, wake and rise

We are marching in the light of God